THE LONG AND
THE SHORT OF IT

One of Kannada literature's foremost contemporary writers, **Devanura Mahadeva** is also a public intellectual whose force of conviction and uncompromising integrity has placed him at the centre of social conversations.

In high school, Devanura was drawn to the Rashtriya Swayamsevak Sangh, primarily because of their 'Hindu ondu' (all Hindus are one) slogan, which to his young ears was a call to equality. What he discovered within the RSS—caste prejudice, anti-Muslim hatred, displeasure at inter-caste marriages—caused him to leave some years later, while he was finishing his pre-university degree. An active member of the socialist activities inaugurated by Ram Manohar Lohia and Jayaprakash Narayan, he took an active part in the resistance to the Emergency in the mid-1970s. In 1977, he co-founded Dalit Sangharsh Samiti, which launched a major Dalit movement in Karnataka. As part of his political engagement, Devanura was instrumental to the founding, in 2005, of the Sarvodaya Karnataka Party—a rare experiment in the country to bring the farmer and Dalit movements together—which later merged with Swaraj India in 2017. He was among the public figures who returned their awards in 2015, protesting the growing intolerance in India; in his case, the Padma Shri and the Sahitya Akademi Award.

Devanura's output as a writer is a small, intense corpus, with every work creating ripples across the Kannada literary firmament. From his short story collection, *Dyavanuru* (1973), published while he was an MA student, to his novel *Kusumabale* (1988), for which he received the Sahitya Akademi Award, or his novella 'Odalala' (1979), every piece of his work is a recognised classic. Published in 2012, *Yedege Bidda Akshara*, a collection of his non-fiction writings, has seen over twenty-five reprints. His latest work, *RSS: Aala Mattu Agala* (2022), became an instant classic, selling over a lakh copies in Kannada and tens of thousands of copies in other languages that it has been translated into.

S.R. Ramakrishna is a Bengaluru-based journalist. His translations include Krupakar and Senani's *Birds, Beasts and Bandits* (Penguin, 2011), Siddalingaiah's *A Word With You, World* (Navayana, 2013) and U.R. Ananthamurthy's *Suragi* (Oxford University Press, 2017).

eka

First published in Kannada in 2022 as *Aala Mattu Agala*

First published in English as *RSS: The Long and the Short of It* in 2022 by Eka, an imprint of Westland Books, a division of Nasadiya Technologies Private Limited.

No. 269/2B, First Floor, 'Irai Arul', Vimalraj Street, Nethaji Nagar, Allappakkam Main Road, Maduravoyal, Chennai 600095

Westland, the Westland logo, Eka and the Eka logo are the trademarks of Nasadiya Technologies Private Limited, or its affiliates.

ISBN: 9789395767163

10 9 8 7 6 5 4 3 2 1

Typeset by Jojy Philip, New Delhi 110 015
Printed at Thomson Press (India) Ltd.

CONTENTS

FOREWORD

Ramachandra Guha

I have never met Devanura Mahadeva, and I do not read Kannada. Nonetheless, I admire him greatly, my admiration based on statements by him reported in the press from time to time, and on a talk I heard him deliver in person. This was in Manipal in 1994, and it was translated for the audience by U.R. Ananthamurthy. The talk explained why the posthumous rivalry between Ambedkar and Gandhi erected by ideologues was deeply unhelpful to our present predicament. Later, back in Bengaluru, the literary scholar D.R. Nagaraj told me about the deep influence Devanura had on his own thought and writing. Nagaraj's own brilliant book, *The Flaming Feet*, took further this idea that India needed, and still needs, both Ambedkar and Gandhi. As Devanura himself put it, in an interview he gave Amrita Dutta in the *Indian Express* in 2020, 'If it is our understanding that it is the Savarnas who need to change if India has to liberate itself from caste, then Gandhi is necessary. In the fight for Dalit civil rights, Ambedkar is absolutely necessary. Hence, I say that both should be brought together.'

In the Kannada literary world, Devanura first made his name through short stories and a novella that received wide acclaim. He has since won respect for his political integrity and his moral courage, for his refusal to succumb to the seductions of state patronage and for his identification with the discriminated and the oppressed. He is a passionate advocate of inter-faith harmony, his commitment to pluralism witnessed most recently in his going to a market in Mysuru to buy and eat halal meat when a ban on the product was sought to be imposed by thugs of a Hindutva persuasion.

When I asked the distinguished Kannada novelist and editor Vivek Shanbhag for an assessment of Devanura's work, he wrote back: 'Devanura's stories are a master class in fiction writing. They depict a dense world of joy, oppression, hunger, caste dynamics, innocence of the oppressed and their protest, strong bonds within a family, and state violence. He has marvellously dealt with all this without uttering any words that we normally associate with these realities. This is his politics and the power of his art. It is inclusive and not limited to Dalits. It compels us to see holistically.'

Shanbhag further remarked that 'as a thinker, Devanura has provided the moral and ethical strength that the Dalit movement in Karnataka needed. However, as I have already said, his politics is never limited to Dalits. This is why his thoughts on Gandhi and Ambedkar are so important in the current context. He is undoubtedly one of our country's major living public intellectuals.'

In July this year, Devanura Mahadeva published a pamphlet outlining his views on the Rashtriya Swayamsevak Sangh (RSS). A week after it was printed, the website *The News Minute* reported: 'A critical exploration of the RSS, the book has been flying off the shelves since its release, prompting the state's rightwing ecosystem to unleash all its arms to discredit both the book and its author.'[1] Members of Parliament of the ruling Bharatiya Janata Party, as well as those who pass as 'intellectuals' on that side of the political spectrum, unburdened themselves with a torrent of abuse aimed at the author. No matter; the pamphlet sold tens of thousands of copies, being discussed and debated in the farthest corners of the state.

Happily for those of us who do not read Kannada, Devanura's pamphlet is now to appear in other languages, including Tamil, Telugu and Malayalam. It is a great privilege for me to here introduce the English translation, which is the handiwork of S.R. Ramakrishna, an accomplished translator who has previously rendered into English, among other works, the autobiography of the poet Siddalingaiah.

In his preface, Devanura says that through this pamphlet he wishes 'to look closely at the true nature and objectives of the Rashtriya

Swayamsevak Sangh'. Intriguingly, he compares the organisation to a magician, who 'excels at hypnotism' and is 'a master of disguise'.

The main text begins with quotations from the two thinkers who have shaped Hindutva as it is today, M.S. Golwalkar and V.D. Savarkar. Here we find Golwalkar justifying the caste system and its inbuilt hierarchies, on the grounds that they have scriptural sanction, and Savarkar urging worship of the Manusmriti, notwithstanding the fact that its endorsement of caste and gender inequalities is so antithetical to the Indian Constitution. The Savarkar quote is especially telling: '*Manusmriti* is that scripture which is most worshipable after Vedas for our Hindu Nation and which from ancient times has become the basis of our culture-customs, thought and practice. This book for centuries has codified the spiritual and divine march of our nation. Even today the rules which are followed by crores of Hindus in their lives and practice are based on *Manusmriti*. Today *Manusmriti* is Hindu Law. That is fundamental.'

A little later in the pamphlet, Devanura quotes Golwalkar as calling the federal system of a union of states 'poisonous', and urging instead a unitary political system based on the homogenising principle of 'One Country, One State, One Legislature, One Executive'. Further quotations remind us of Golwalkar's admiration for Hitler and the Nazis, and of what they did to make their nation and race 'pure' through the purging of Germany's Jewish population.

In his pamphlet, Devanura draws our attention to the crudity of what passes for thinking in the RSS. The Sangh's Bible, as it were, is a book of Golwalkar's, entitled *Bunch of Thoughts*, but, as Devanura writes, '[i]f you search inside this book for anything that could be considered a "thought", or "chintane", you will find absolutely nothing. What it offers is only a set of random, dangerous beliefs, and that too from a bygone age.' (Having read the book closely myself, I entirely concur with this judgement.) The RSS's ideology is so narrow-minded that, as Devanura remarks, '[f]orget about anyone else, no sensible Brahmin even can accept this devilish view of the past that the RSS presents.' Animated by archaic notions of patriarchy and upper-caste pride, the RSS 'seems to believe that Dalits and women are immature, lacking in intelligence and individuality, and incapable of making their own decisions'.

Devanura writes from the perspective of a defender of the Indian Constitution. For all the lip service that leaders of the RSS and the BJP pay to that document, in truth they are deeply averse to its core tenets, such as pluralism, caste and gender equality, freedom of speech and federalism. Devanura goes so far as to suggest that '[t]he more they damage the Indian Constitution, the more victorious they feel'. He continues: 'To destroy the Constitution, the RSS and its affiliates are committing unspeakable acts. They are playing games they shouldn't be playing. And these aren't just one or two! They are waging a war to overturn the federalism that binds the states and the union government, and that constitutes the bedrock of the Constitution. For the RSS, diversity causes disintegration; it is a "poisonous seed". Golwalkar says "Any talk of federalism must be buried deep. Let's rewrite the Constitution to put in place a unitary government". Devanura remarks that since coming to power in 2014, '[t]he BJP has offered Golwalkar its guru dakshina by burying federalism, by stifling to death the federal system that constitutes a critical part of the Constitution'.

He argues that 'Hitler's authoritarian idea, of one flag, one national ideology, one race and one leader, is an ideal for the RSS.' Thus, since 2014, '[u]nder Narendra Modi's reign, the judiciary, the executive and the media, as also other autonomous institutions, are finding it hard to breathe. In its dream run, the RSS has started taking control of all domains of society. In other words, it is bringing about one leadership for everything—party, society, culture, administration … everything.'

While the RSS's hatred of Muslims and suspicion of Christians are well known and widely documented, Devanura also brings to light the Sangh's attempt to suppress and tame religions of Indic origin that (in common with Christianity and Islam) sought to reject the caste system. He writes that '[t]he RSS tries to pull out the teeth and nails of Jaina, Bouddha, Sikh,

Lingayat and other dharmas that were born in India and rejected the Chaturvarna order. Saying "This is all ours", it swallows them up and subsumes them into the Chaturvarna order.'

Of the religious polarisation promoted by the Sangh, Devanura observes: 'Posing as a representative of the larger Hindu majority, this Hindutva sect has cast a spell on innumerable liberal Hindu communities and filled them with hatred against Muslims and Christians. Its aim is to draw them into its fold by declaring a war of hate against those religions.'

Devanura also highlights the scant regard for the truth, the distortions of the historical record and the fake news that the Hindu Right has long been known for, now amplified by WhatsApp and Facebook. As he puts it, 'Falsehood is their family deity.' He examines the falsehoods propagated in textbooks issued by BJP governments, which are controlled by the RSS and which seek to poison the minds of our children with hatred of Indians who do not happen to be Hindus.

To his credit, Devanura acknowledges that political forces other than the RSS and the BJP have also contributed to democratic decline in India. As he observes: 'When you look at India's political parties, you find three categories: (1) a single-person-led party, (2) a family-controlled party and (3) a party led by an organisation that pays no heed to Constitutional norms. All three are detrimental to democracy.' However, it is the BJP that is in power at the Centre and in many major states. Given the dominant status the Sangh Parivar occupies today, it was imperative that Devanura focus on the pernicious social ideology of the RSS and its dangerous political articulation through the BJP.

Devanura also talks of the false promises made by the lifelong RSS pracharak Narendra Modi when he became prime minister in 2014, about, among other things, the return of black money, the doubling of farm incomes and the generation of millions of jobs. These promises have remained wholly unfulfilled. Instead, economic inequalities and disparities of wealth have grown alarmingly. The principal beneficiaries of Narendra Modi's prime ministership have been

It is thus that Devanura ends with a gentle call to action, a plea to all those who oppose the RSS and the BJP to 'flow collectively as one river', by coming together on a common platform to restore the foundations of the Republic and rescue it from being further ravaged by the fanatics on the right.

PREFACE

As we begin…

This little book is an attempt to look closely at the true nature and objectives of the Rashtriya Swayamsevak Sangh (RSS), a step towards making people aware of where the organisation is leading our country, and to reveal the difference between its true colours and how it is perceived.

Make people aware, yes, but how? In our folklore, we hear the story of the magician who breathes his life into a parrot, hides it in a cave beyond the seven seas, and goes on to wreak mindless havoc in the world. Needless to say, he is a magician. And a master of disguise to boot. His forms are many. He excels at hypnotism, too. Apparently, nothing can harm him. Because the parrot, which carries his life breath, is safe in a faraway cave. The first thing to do in such a situation, if we set out to do anything at all, is to find where this life breath is hidden. A search becomes necessary. As part of such a search, I peered into the old, musty well of the RSS. What I saw was terrifying. What this booklet contains is only a glimpse. If it offers even a little inspiration to those who wish to write more expansively about the RSS in the future, that alone would make it worthwhile.

1

Where is the RSS's life breath hidden away?

Dr Hedgewar[1] is the founding father of the RSS. He considered Savarkar[2] his guru, philosopher and guide. Golwalkar[3] was the chief of the RSS for a long time. Now, let us consider some passages from Golwalkar and Savarkar.

Golwalkar's God:[4]

> The first and the most fundamental aspect is the urge for realisation of the Supreme Reality permeating the entire Universe—whatever the name given to it. Or in simple words, it is 'to realise God.' But where is God? How can we know Him? How does He look? What are His appearances […] The description that He is nirakar (without form), nirguna (without attributes) and all that leads us nowhere.

Various ways of worship are also evolved. […] But all this does not satisfy us who are full of activity. We want a 'living' God. […]

Hence our forefathers, understanding the limitations of the human mind and intellect, said, 'humanity' and all that is all right, but before one can rise to that state, one should take a view of the Almighty with certain limitations as it were, which one can understand, feel and serve. The Hindu People, they said, is the *Virāt Purusha*, the Almighty manifesting Himself. Though they did not use the word 'Hindu', it is clear from the following description of the Almighty in *Pursha Sūkta* wherein it is stated that the sun and moon are his eyes, the stars and the skies are created from His *nābhi* (navel) and

ब्राह्मणोऽस्य मुखमासीद् बाहू राजन्यः कृतः ।
ऊरू तदस्य यद्वैश्यः पद्भ्याँ शूद्रोऽअजायत ॥

(Brahmin is the head. King the arms. Vaishya the thighs and Shudra the feet.) This means that the people who have this fourfold arrangement, i.e., the Hindu People, is our God.

The Manudharmashastra in Savarkar's view:[5]

> *Manusmriti* is that scripture which is most worshipable after Vedas for our Hindu Nation and which from ancient times has become the basis of our culture-customs, thought and practice. This book for centuries has codified the spiritual and divine march of our nation. Even today the rules which are followed by crores of Hindus in their lives and practice are based on *Manusmriti*. Today *Manusmriti* is Hindu Law. That is fundamental.

Noting that people taking pride in Hindu traditions exist everywhere, Golwalkar writes:[6]

> In [the] Philippines a marble statue of Manu is placed in the Court Hall with the inscription: 'The first, the greatest and the wisest lawgiver of mankind.'

On Hitler and Nazism, Golwakar writes:

> German race pride has now become the topic of the day. To keep up the purity of the Race and its culture, Germany shocked the world by her purging the country of the semitic Races—the Jews. Race pride at its highest has been manifested here. Germany has also

shown how well nigh impossible it is for Races and cultures, having differences going to the root, to be assimilated into one united whole, a good lesson for us in Hindusthan to learn and profit by.[7] [...]

It is worth bearing well in mind how these old Nations solve their minorities problem. They do not undertake to recognise any separate elements in their polity. Emigrants have to get themselves naturally assimilated in the principal mass of population, the National Race, by adopting its culture and language and sharing in its aspirations, by losing all consciousness of their separate existence, forgetting their foreign origin. If they do not do so, they live merely as outsiders, bound by all the codes and conventions of the Nation, at the sufferance of the Nation and deserving of no special protection, far less any privilege or rights. There are only two courses open to the foreign elements, either to merge themselves in the national race and adopt its culture, or to live at its mercy so long as the national race may allow them to do so and to quit the country at the sweet will of the national race. That is the only sound view on the minorities problem. That is the only logical and correct solution. That alone keeps the national life healthy and undisturbed. That alone keeps the Nation safe from the danger of a cancer developing into its body politic of the creation of a state within the state.[8]

Savarkar on Nazism:[9]

The very fact that Germany or Italy has so wonderfully recovered and grown so powerful as never before at the touch of Nazi or Fascist magical wand is enough to prove that those political 'isms' were the most congenial tonics their health demanded.

Golwalkar on the Constitution and federalism:
The Poisonous Seed

That the framers of our present Constitution also were not firmly rooted in the conviction of our single homogeneous nationhood is evident from the federal structure of our Constitution. Our country is now described as a Union of states. Those that were merely provinces in the former set-up are now given the status of States, with many exclusive powers. In fact, it was the fragmentation of our single national life in the past into so many exclusive political units that sowed the seeds of national disintegration and defeat. The present federal structure has in it the same seeds of disruption, which are already sprouting.[10] [...]

Towards this end the most important and effective step will be to bury deep for good all talk of a federal structure of our country's Constitution, to sweep away the existence of all 'autonomous' or semi-autonomous 'states' within the one State viz., Bharat and proclaim 'One Country, One State, One Legislature, One Executive' with no trace of fragmentational, regional, sectarian, linguistic or other types of pride being given a scope for playing havoc with our integrated harmony. Let the Constitution be re-examined and re-drafted, so as to establish the unitary form of Government.[11]

On freedom, Golwakar writes:

In fact, protection and propagation of our national life-values i.e., our *dharma* and *samskriti*, have always been held in our historical tradition as the raison d'etre of *swatantratā*.[12]

Golwalkar on what inspires the RSS:[13]

RSS, inspired by one flag, one leader and one ideology is lighting the flame of Hindutva in each and every corner of this great land.

2

The documents speak in these ways…

The previous chapter, titled 'Where is the RSS's life breath hidden away?', gives you a drift of what is contained in the writings of Golwalkar and Savarkar. Only the documents have spoken there. Forget anyone else, no sensible Brahmin even can accept this devilish view of the past that the RSS presents.

Golwalkar had titled his book *Bunch of Thoughts*. Its Kannada translation is called *Chintanaganga*. If you search this book for anything that could be considered a 'thought', or 'chintane', you will find absolutely nothing. What it offers is only a set of random, dangerous beliefs, and that too from a bygone age.

In the first place, the social order, as contained in the Purusha Sukta,[1] is in itself God for the RSS. For them, that social order, with the Brahmin as head, Kshatriya as arms, Vaishya as thighs and Shudra as feet, is the embodiment of God. Golwalkar calls this order 'a living God'. This belief is the foundation of the RSS. In fact, for them, God is manifest in this very belief.

So, really, all we need to do in order to understand how this God works is to look at our own heads, arms, thighs and feet. The head is the brain, and the arms, thighs and feet obey the brain's orders. If this is applied to society, the Kshatriyas must rule in accordance with what the Brahmins say. The Vaishyas as thighs must trade in tandem, and the Shudras as feet must serve everyone else. This, for the RSS, is social justice and social harmony. This is their Supreme Being, their living God.

Aiming to cast this idea of God into the tender minds of little children, the BJP, a part of the RSS family, is out to make the Bhagavad Gita, where the God incarnate Krishna himself is said to have proclaimed, 'I created the four-fold varnas', a school textbook in the states under its rule.[2] When was the Gita written? Was there a mention of the four-fold varnas in the original text? Was the Gita an interpolation? If indeed it was, when did the interpolation take place?

Swami Vivekananda says of the Gita's authenticity:[3]

Another point is, the book, Gita, had not been much known to the generality of people before Shankarâchârya made it famous by writing his great commentary on it. Long before that, there was current, according to many, the commentary on it by Bodhâyana [...] not a copy even of that Bodhâyana Bhashya could I find while travelling throughout India. It is said that even Ramanuja compiled his Bhashya from a worm-eaten manuscript which he happened to find. When even this great Bodhâyana Bhashya on the Vedanta-Sutras is so much enshrouded in the darkness of uncertainty, it is simply useless to try to establish the existence of the Bodhayana Bhashya on the Gita. Some infer that Shankarâchârya was the author of the Gita, and that it was he who foisted it into the body of the Mahabharata.

Is Vivekananda's word not enough to show that there was an interpolation in the Gita to convince people that the inequality and slavery intrinsic to the Chaturvarna order were divinely ordained? Details like these don't matter to the RSS. History is whatever they believe, the puranas are whatever they say. They don't want the truth. For the RSS, their beliefs are the truth. Their beliefs must shape the present. The more they damage the Indian Constitution, the more victorious they feel.

The petty Hindutva sect that is devoted to the Chaturvarna order—and which wishes to see a child born in India as a universal human, a vishvamanava, shackled by jati and varna all its life—finds the civilised, humane Indian Constitution a nightmare. The Constitution robs it of its sleep. To destroy the Constitution, the RSS and its affiliates are committing unspeakable acts. They are playing games they shouldn't be playing. And these aren't just one or two! They are waging a war to overturn the federalism that binds the states and the union government, and constitutes the bedrock of the Constitution. For the RSS, diversity causes disintegration; it is a 'poisonous seed'. Golwalkar says, '[T]he most important and effective step will be to bury deep for good all talk of a federal structure of our country's Constitution … Let the Constitution be re-examined and re-drafted, so as to establish this Unitary form of Government …'[4] Furthermore, Hitler's authoritarian idea, of one flag, one national ideology, one race and one leader, is an ideal for the RSS.

Let us also keep this in mind: even Indira Gandhi of the Congress was a dictator for a while. While she sought to muffle the media, neither her party nor her supporters tried to take ownership of it, as their counterparts in government are doing today. People who protested the Emergency were heroes, but protestors against Modi's government are considered anti-national. During Indira Gandhi's short-lived dictatorship, the judiciary, the executive and the media had not lost their vitality to the extent they have now. Under Narendra Modi's reign, the judiciary, the executive and the media, as also other autonomous institutions, are finding it hard to breathe. In its dream run, the RSS has started taking control of all domains of society. In other words, it is bringing about one leadership for everything—party, society, culture, administration ... everything. This is absolute dictatorship. It is important to remember this.

Whether it be the desire to set up a Chaturvarna social order, adopt Manudharmashastra as the Constitution, or make Sanskrit the lingua franca of India, all of them reveal a conspiracy to dig up the grave, stir the past awake and bring it to bear today. Golwalkar talks about the need to use Hindi as a first step to making Sanskrit the lingua franca in India.[5]

> As a solution, problem of lingua franca, till the time Sanskrit takes that place, we shall have to give priority to Hindi on the score of convenience.

The third important belief of the RSS is the supremacy of the Aryan race. This is a deep-seated obsession of theirs. Hitler, the cruel dictator of that special Aryan breed, is himself the role model for the RSS. Addressing the students of Gujarat University, Golwalkar said:[6]

Today experiments in cross-breeding are made only on animals. But the courage to make such experiments on human beings is not shown even by the so-called modern scientist of today. If some human cross-breeding is seen today it is the result not of scientific experiments but of carnal lust. Now let us see the experiments our ancestors made in this sphere. In an effort to better the human species through cross-breeding the Namboodri Brahamanas of the North were settled in Kerala and a rule was laid down that the eldest son of a Namboodri family could marry only the daughter of Vaishya, Kshatriya or Shudra communities of Kerala. Another still more courageous rule was that the first off-spring of a married woman of any class must be fathered by a Namboodri Brahman and then she could beget children by her husband. Today this experiment will be called adultery but it was not so, as it was limited to the first child.

Golwalkar had narrated the story tellingly and with specific details. As if he had seen everything with his own eyes. But here is the travesty. After Golwalkar shared his idea of eugenics at Gujarat University, and the RSS's official weekly, *Organiser*, reported his speech, he took back his words. Only, by then, it had already been documented and recorded. The question was whether what he described was a fact of history, or whether it was just a figment of the imagination. If Golwalkar retracted what he had said, it is possible that he was admitting to a falsehood, a fabrication. When such incidents occur, we should express regret over them. Instead, the RSS looks at them with pride and treats them as tradition. Their narratives have seeded the growth of falsehood everywhere. Such lies, intended to flourish until they are checked and exposed, are spreading like weeds across the length and breadth of India on WhatsApp and Facebook, and in the news media and everyday conversations.

This method of creating false stories is Golwalkar's contribution. Humanism and the ways of civilisation seem to have left the RSS untouched, which, along with its affiliates, is relentlessly sowing such weed-like lies. Relentlessly.

15

3

It continues…

The RSS tries to pull out the teeth and nails of Jaina, Bouddha, Sikh, Lingayat and other dharmas that were born in India and rejected the Chaturvarna order. Saying 'They are part of us', it swallows them up and subsumes them into the Chaturvarna order. On another front, it unleashes its groups and attacks Islam and Christianity, religions that refuse to allow the Chaturvarna Hindu order to swallow them up. These attacks come in a variety of forms, and in many guises. They are not new. The game of disguise and deception is perhaps something the RSS was born with.

Here is an example. In a letter dated 14 March 1948, soon-to-be president Dr Rajendra Prasad wrote to Home Minister Sardar Vallabhbhai Patel,

'I am told that RSS people have a plan of creating trouble. They have got a number of men dressed as Muslims and looking like Muslims who are to create trouble with the Hindus by attacking them and thus inciting the Hindus. Similarly, there will be some Hindus among them who will attack Muslims and thus incite Muslims. The result of this kind of trouble amongst the Hindus and Muslims will be to create a conflagration.'[1] If they were doing all this back then, what must they be doing now? How many more disguises they must be wearing these days! And who knows how many more are to come?

The smear campaign against Tipu Sultan is a good example of how the RSS and its progeny create falsehoods. Tipu ruled the state of Mysore between 1782 and 1799. The RSS ideologues claim that, in Kodagu, he converted 69,000 Hindus to Islam. If you look at the population figures in the gazetteer, and regardless of how you do the math, the Kodagu province had fewer than 69,000 people then. If the RSS claim were true, wouldn't Kodagu be populated only by Muslims today? But the Muslim population in

Kodagu is just 15 per cent.[2] The story of Tipu's hatred of Hindus is a planted lie. The tragedy is that this weed-like lie is thriving, and the RSS and its affiliates are reaping the harvest of it. When you consider all this, it becomes clear that they have no God within. Falsehood is their family deity. It looks like these manufacturers of falsehood have hanged their conscience.

The main reason for the RSS's hatred of Islam and Christianity is that they refuse to dissolve into the Chaturvarna order. That fact makes these two religions hard for the Chaturvarna Hindu sect to accept. The thinking in the RSS is to make these religions submit at any cost, and render them lifeless by depriving them of any rights in India. As we saw earlier, Golwalkar believed Hitler's Nazism held for Hindus 'a good lesson' on the need to maintain racial purity and ensure that all foreigners are assimilated into 'the national race', or make them 'live at its mercy'. Such is his vision, an imitation of Hitler's anti-Semitism.

But in truth, have all Muslims and Christians in India migrated from foreign lands? Isn't it true that a majority of people following these faiths are those who converted from Hindu communities to escape the debilitating Chaturvarna order and the caste system? Following the arrival of Islam in India, the first to convert—lured by power, status, ministerships and military positions—were mostly north Indian Aryan Brahmins, weren't they?[3] Aren't Aryan Brahmins found among the Muslims settled in Pakistan, a country the RSS detests? The RSS wants nothing to do with these truths. Posing as a representative of the larger Hindu majority, this Hindutva sect has cast a spell on innumerable liberal Hindu communities and filled them with hatred against Muslims and Christians. Its aim is to draw them into its fold by declaring a war of hate against those religions.

The RSS wants a war of hate. The majority community of former Shudras, made up of countless castes and sects, who fall victim to hate and participate in the war, will have its wings quietly clipped. In this war of hate, the rights of these former Shudras will be snatched away. The Scheduled Castes, Scheduled Tribes and Backward Classes have been asserting their Constitutional rights, demanding their due in education, employment and politics, and organising to struggle for them only because they have had clear caste and community identities. Amid calls of 'all Hindus are one', when these former Shudras, now shorn of their identities, enter the furnace of the Hindu–Muslim war of hate as Hindus, their Constitutional rights are obscured. It would be as if they were all caught in the net of the petty Chaturvarna sect of Hindutva, and as a result, the dictates of the Brahmins, the head, would decide how the Kshatriyas as the arms rule, the Vaishyas as the thighs conduct their trade, and the Shudras, like their ancestors, serve the others and crawl through their lives after losing their Constitutional rights.[4] India would then appear like it has returned to the past.

When one looks at the RSS from the inside, a couple of other aspects need to be noticed. It is not a solitary organisation trying to wake up the ghosts of the past and make them real in the present. It has also shaken awake its young offspring. The details are explained in a book titled

Param Vaibhav Ke Path Par, published in 1997 by Suruchi Prakashan, a publishing house that publishes RSS literature. It lists among the brood about forty organisations, such as the Bharatiya Janata Party (BJP), Akhil Bharatiya Vidyarthi Parishad, Hindu Jagran Manch, Sanskar Bharti, Vishwa Hindu Parishad and Bajrang Dal. This was the number in 1996. Who knows how many more it has spawned since? Even the federation called Dharam Sansad comes under the RSS. Sri Rama Sene, founded by an expelled member of the Bajrang Dal in Karntaka, is also among them. These are the friends and relatives of the RSS. When such groups go on the rampage and earn notoriety, it is customary for the RSS to say it has no connection with them. But we shouldn't be deceived. They share an umbilical link with the RSS.

The most terrible of all is the manner in which the RSS tames the volunteers who come into its fold. Golwalkar says:[5]

> If we say that we are part of the organization and accept its discipline then selectiveness *(chunna)* has no place in life. Do what is told.

If told to play kabaddi, play kabaddi, told to hold meeting then meeting… For instance some of our friends were asked to go and work in politics that does not mean that they have great interest or inspiration for it. They don't die for politics like fish without water. If they are told to withdraw from politics then also there is no objection. Their discretion *(vivek)* is just not required.

Golwalkar rules out allowing swayamsevaks any discretion. Choices, he says, don't exist for them. This is distressing because the RSS pulls young children into its organisational fold. It doesn't make humans out of them; instead, it creates inhuman robots called swayamsevaks. How do we rescue children caught in the jaws of the RSS?

All kinds of communal fanaticism rage today, even though Hindu, Muslim, Christian and other faiths are all born of the same mother. Their outward forms might look different, but at heart, they are the same. Fanaticism anywhere devours humanism. The only hope now is that the majority, watching everything silently so far, will be outraged and refuse to cooperate. Otherwise, fanaticism will pluck out the eyes of its own people to render them blind. It will then pull out their brains and rob them of reason. Next, it will consume their hearts and make them cruel. Finally, fanaticism will demand human sacrifice. This is what is increasingly happening today. We have to act quickly and protect our children's eyes, brains and hearts from the claws of fanaticism.

The vast Hindu community shouldn't let this minority Chaturvarna sect, a cow-faced tiger, get away with such inhuman actions. It must speak out during this crisis, and not sit watching it all quietly. Starting with the Adivasis, and including the Brahmins, the multitude of castes forming the humane majority of Hindu society must act now.

4

And now, in the present…

Today, the BJP, one of the RSS's many offspring, holds the reins of power at the centre and also in some states. In Karnataka, too, it has managed to seize power, doing this, that and the other.

In the early Seventies, the RSS—and the Jana Sangh, the predecessor of today's BJP—wriggled into Jayaprakash Narayan's (JP's) movement against Indira Gandhi's corrupt misrule. With that, its fortunes changed. Rejected by society thus far, it started gaining acceptance. At the time of joining the Janata Party, formed just then, the chief of the RSS had promised JP that members of the Jana Sangh would give up their dual membership. Prominent among those who made this promise were A.B. Vajpayee, L.K. Advani and

Balasaheb Deoras, then the chief of the RSS. JP, who had regarded them as tall leaders, took their word at face value. However, even as leaders with RSS roots mixed with the members of the Janata Party, they didn't give up their dual membership. The promise was broken. The RSS had won JP's trust only to let him down. In his twilight years, JP recalled what had transpired, and despaired, 'They betrayed my trust.'

During the Emergency, the Delhi district magistrate had ordered JP's arrest under the Maintenance of Internal Security Act,[1] and transferred him to the Chandigarh district jail for security reasons. Given how fragile his health was, JP was confined in the Post Graduate Institute of Medical Research, the ward and guest house of which were notified as a prison under the Criminal Procedure Code. G.M. Devasahayam was the district magistrate in Chandigarh then, and therefore his custodian in jail. He became close to JP in the course of their interaction, a relationship that continued even after JP was released. Devasahayam shares these details in an interview with Ajaz Ashraf.[2]

Since then, the saga of the RSS and the BJP's betrayal has spread across the length and breadth of the country. The BJP portrays Pakistan as a permanent enemy, blames it even for minor squabbles here, pits one community against another, creates an atmosphere of fear, and on occasion, even starts disturbances and points fingers at the Muslims. In short, the party has ruined the peace all around, and risen to power amid the ensuing confusion, suspicion and hatred. Now, the vast, richly abundant and diverse Hindu religion, made up of hundreds of sects and half a dozen dharmas, has been pushed to despair, much like JP, to say, 'Even I was deceived.'

How many promises the BJP made before coming to power, how many disguises it wore! Not just one or two. Narendra Damodardas Modi declared that all Indians would get Rs 15 lakh in their bank accounts if the black money stashed away by Indians in foreign banks was brought back.[3] Innocent Indians believe it could still happen, since Modi had said so himself. Who has received this money? If indeed the black money did come back, what happened to it? Modi also said he would create crores of jobs every year.[4] He has created unemployment like never before.[5] Who is to ask him, who is to tell him? He said he would double farmers' incomes. But he didn't spare even their existing incomes. In fact, he caused them to crash.[6] He lets nothing survive. He lives by selling public assets to private parties.[7] He has taken foreign debt to never-before highs.[8]

When you look at all this, you fear that Modi will push the country to bankruptcy with fantastic promises and colourful words. It doesn't bother him that unemployment is rising, it doesn't bother him that prices are skyrocketing. His rule is such that it ignites hatred between communities—it makes citizens seethe with hatred, and then makes them fall asleep by feeding them more hatred. Even those who voted the BJP to power have reached a point of despair.

At the root of all this is *the degeneration of people's power*. The people's representatives are not responsive to the joys and sorrows of those who chose them. When you look at India's political parties, you will see that they can be classified into three categories: (1) single-person-led party politics, (2) family-controlled party politics and (3) politics steered by an organisation that pays no heed to Constitutional norms. All three are detrimental to democracy. Parties found across India fall into one or the other of these categories. The BJP, controlled by an organisation that shows little regard for the Constitution, now steers the country. Just as representatives elected from the first two categories are more loyal to the individuals and families that control them than to the people who elected them, representatives from a party controlled by an organisation that is indifferent to the Constitution are more loyal to that organisation than to their voters or even their party. This is more dangerous to democracy than anything else. Today, there can be no other reason why the BJP legislators, parliamentarians and ministers, leaders big and small, climb over each other to make a noise to impress the RSS, which regulates their party.

We should note another feature of party politics when it is regulated by an organisation with scant regard for the Constitution. Prime Minister Modi, who won a majority for the BJP, is projected as a strong leader. But he is only an utsava murti, a replica of the temple deity taken out during a procession. The real deity sits in Nagpur, inside the RSS shrine. The utsava murti dazzles everyone across the length and breadth of the country. It is hailed everywhere. The qualifications for an utsava murti are the ability to put up a show and the canniness to give an emotional colour to things that spin out of control, and create a commotion, and thus take attention away from the problem. It should also know how to mesmerise people and remain totally loyal to the deity ensconced in the sanctum sanctorum. That's all it takes.

Don't we see all of this today? Another potential tragedy for democracy is that the leader of the party, already regulated by an organisation that cares little for the Constitution, is decided by the deity inside the sanctum sanctorum. It is like a priest handing a flower to a supplicant. Everything is a puppet show! If a new puppet dances better to a given tune than the current one, and shows more colour, dazzle, devotion and cunning, it enters the stage wearing a mask of strength or astuteness. It becomes the leader. The puppet that played the leader earlier is flung aside. However strong, no leader who refuses to dance as instructed survives for long. Just imagine, this is the plight of those elected by citizens. It is a frightening situation. And it is more harmful to democracy than anything else could be. A perilous development.

All of these factors come together to make the lives of people miserable. If the prime minister—and leader of the BJP, a party controlled by an organisation that is heedless of the Constitution—had any competence, unemployment would have come down. Prices would be under control. He wouldn't be running the government by selling public assets. He wouldn't be increasing our foreign debt. He wouldn't have pulled out the nails and teeth of India's autonomous institutions and made them dull.

Let's now take a look at the dance of blind money[9] in Modi's regime. Before the pandemic broke out, in mid-March 2020, the wealth of Gautam Adani, a Gujarati, was Rs 66,696 crores. In mid-March 2022, as life was returning to normal after the pandemic, it had jumped to Rs 6,90,840 crores. Over the next six months, it went up to Rs 12,16,985 crores.[10] Adani was listed as the second richest individual in the world in September 2022.[11] Similarly, the wealth of Mukesh Ambani, also from Gujarat, has gone up exponentially. In just over two years, by September 2022, it had gone up to Rs 7.2 lakh crores.[12] Of course, other Indian billionaires are thriving, too.

How is the income of an average Indian calculated? The wealth of these billionaires is combined with the earnings of those in straitened circumstances, and then divided by the total number of Indians. What does an average income then mean for the poor? The sky-high wealth of the rich is a figure that Indians only hear about. A higher average income doesn't translate into food for the hungry. India's rank in the hunger index is also rising, in tandem with the wealth of the billionaires. This is what it is, the blind gamble of blind money.

How many things do we talk about? Because of this grim inequality and imbalance, India is plunging and fluttering wildly like a kite with a snapped string. Still, it looks like this government exists only to provide concessions, tax cuts and loan waivers to the rich.[13] It is writing off loans worth thousands of crores, putting aside even the expectation that the money will return some day, so that it can lend again to the same rich people.[14] The number of the poor people is doubling. For whom does this government exist? The situation today is that the people are despairing, holding their heads in their hands. It's strength sapped, India is sighing.

5

Where does it end?

Come what may, and regardless of how badly citizens suffer, and even if it means the country is broken into fragments, the BJP is chanting the mantra of patriotism to bring in new laws and amend the ones already in place. The intention is to slip into them the Chaturvarna system and Manudharmashastra, to destroy the Indian Constitution, propagate intolerance towards Islam and Christianity, and practise Aryan supremacism. These tendencies are easily spotted. The Karnataka Protection of Right to Freedom of Religion Ordinance of 2022 looks like just another law. If you lay bare its insides, you find that it is intended to destroy the Indian Constitution and establish the Manudharmashastra in its place.[1] All of us speak about freedom the way the Constitution envisions it. But the RSS looks at freedom differently. According to RSS's guruji, Golwalkar, '[the] protection and propagation of our national life-values i.e., our *dharma* and *samskriti* have always been held in our historical tradition as the raison d'etre of *swatantrata*'.[2]

For the BJP, a child of the RSS, the words of guru Golwalkar are its Constitution. When he says 'dharma', let us keep in mind, Golwalkar refers to the petty sect that propagates the Chaturvarna order, and not to the innumerable, heterogeneous Hindu sects at large. If that petty Hindutva sect gets to stand in for Hinduism, should we see this situation as moral (dharma) or immoral (adharma)? We must ask this question. At least from now on, we must tell the world over and over again that what the RSS calls Hinduism is nothing other than the Chaturvarna sect. If Golwalkar's Chaturvarna order were to be established as the moral order (dharma), then what is to become of the right to personal liberty, the freedom of expression and the freedom of religion provided under the Indian

Constitution? Also, should the most populous groups within the Chaturvarna order of the past, once called the Shudras, become servants all over again? We have to confront these questions with utmost seriousness.

In *Bunch of Thoughts*, Golwalkar says the federal system propounded in the Constitution should be buried. The BJP, the RSS's descendant, has buried the federal system with a single stroke—by introducing the goods and services tax (GST). On the surface, the GST looks like an act of financial reform. But its impact? The states in our federation have surrendered all their powers to the centre. They place all their wealth at the feet of the centre, and then beg for their share. The BJP has offered Golwalkar its guru dakshina by burying federalism, by stifling the federal system that constitutes a critical part of the Constitution. Now, the 'republic of states' has become weak, and a 'strong centre' has taken its place. Likewise, the conspiracy to make Hindi the link language, as a first step towards making Sanskrit the link language, is already peeping out at us. These are the first steps of a hidden, anti-diversity agenda, enforcing ideas of one nation, one language and one leader, of the superiority of one race and the like.

It is the same story in education too. The RSS first reaches out to strangle education and history. Such is its hatred that the BJP government plans to remove references like this from the Class 6 social studies textbook: 'Tipu Sultan waged many wars against the Britishers. He negotiated with the French to dethrone the British rule in India.'[3] Similarly, it has dropped references to Tipu's initiatives in sericulture, his establishment of a mint, his land reforms, his practice of giving easy loans to farmers, and so on. Likewise, a lesson in the social science textbook of Class 6 titled 'The rise of new religions', which discussed the emergence of Jaina dharma and Bouddha dharma in ancient India, was unpalatable to the BJP, which moved it to a Class 8 lesson under a new title, 'Jaina and Bouddha matagalu (sects)', mischaracterising the Jaina and Bouddha religions as 'sects'. Native Indian religions, such as the Bouddha, Jaina, Sikh and Lingayat dharmas, are hard for this minority Chaturvarna

Hindutva sect to accept. The RSS is constantly trying to annihilate authentic religions that reject the Chaturvarna system.

This is not new. In 1998, when the BJP-led National Democratic Alliance came to power, its human resources minister, Dr Murli Manohar Joshi, introduced 'Paurohitya' (priest craft) and 'Karmakand' (rituals) in the curriculum.[4] In his time, astrology came to be taught at the universities.[5] A lesson spoke about how to beget a male child by performing the putrakameshti yajna ritual. The BJP fills children's heads with mindless thoughts and superstitions. Whenever it is in power, it tries to enforce Golwalkar's injunction about children's education—children who take part in RSS activities need only obey.

Recently, they dropped several topics from the CBSE syllabus—'democracy and diversity', 'the impact of globalisation on agriculture' and two poems by Faiz Ahmed Faiz in the 'Religion, Communalism and Politics—Communalism, Secular State' section.[6] The RSS has given birth to a team whose job is to have lessons removed. It is called 'Shiksha Sanskriti Utthan Nyas'. This body has been pressuring the NCERT to drop lines referring to the killing of 2,000 Muslims during the 2002 Gujarat riots and to former prime minister Manmohan Singh showing grace by seeking forgiveness for the 1984 anti-Sikh riots. That is how they operate. If they can make events witnessed by us vanish, imagine what they can do with a past that we haven't even seen.

At this rate, our textbooks might come to say that Hedgewar, the founder of the RSS who turned away from the freedom movement, and Savarkar, who apologised to the British and is now glorified with the title of 'Veer', got us our independence. For that matter, a myth may be created that Nathuram Godse, who killed Gandhi, was a 'defender of Hindu dharma'. Who knows what yarns the RSS and its affiliates will spin next!

How many things can I talk about? It would suffice to examine the RSS's obsession with Aryan supremacy. They are bringing into circulation the term 'vanavasis' (forest dwellers) in place of 'adivasis' (indigenous dwellers) and 'moola nivasis' (original dwellers). Those who have a history of grabbing everything from the indigenous people are now trying to snatch away their very identity. The reason is simple. As long as terms like 'original dwellers' are around, the 'Aryans' will continue to feel like outsiders in India. A recent DNA study conducted in Rakhigarhi, Haryana, based on remains found in the Indus Valley civilisation site, has found that the people of the Indus civilisation had no Aryan or Vedic blood in their lineage.[7] Shaken by this finding, the RSS has begun calling it the 'Saraswati civilisation' instead of the 'Indus Valley civilisation'. But what is the harm in saying that the Aryans came from beyond our borders? India embraces all children born on its soil as its own. Moreover, in India, Dravidian, Aryan, Islamic, Christian and other bloods are inseparably mixed and can't be told apart. Why can't the RSS just live in the present in peace? It looks like the RSS is suffering from a pathological obsession with Aryan supremacism.

So, to take this further, who are the Sri Rama Sene and Bajrang Dal boys creating disturbances in the name of hijab, halal trading ban and azaan? Aren't they mostly the youth force of the communities at the bottom of society? Wouldn't the country have thrived if they had been given jobs according to their abilities? The BJP, a child of the RSS, wants none of this. For the RSS and BJP, the former Shudras must be foot soldiers, they must remain helpless, they must remain servants as laid down in the Chaturvarna order: this is what is quietly coming to pass here. Isn't this the plight of contract workers? When the farmers' ties with their land are weakened, won't it bring back the servant order made up of landless Shudras? When new positions remain vacant and backlogs in government departments are left unfilled, and jobs are handed over to the private sector where no job reservation exists, aren't the RSS and BJP pushing back communities that benefit from reservation to being Shudra servants? We see the same pattern when the central government cuts down jobs and curtails the rights of workers. Statistics from the Centre for Monitoring Indian Economy show that about two crore women disappeared from the workforce between 2017 and 2022.[8] Is this natural, accidental, or a result of the RSS strategy to keep women confined to their homes? Such questions and doubts arise.

While all this is going on, they are also privatising education and weakening the public education system. As a result, the education of rural children, especially girls, is on the wane. And thus, new kinds of discriminatory systems[9] are now found even in children's education. In effect, all of this will likely take us to a situation, like the one seen in the past Chaturvarna order, where Shudras are considered unfit for education. These are the sorts of things that are underway. This is what we know so far. But the situation makes us wonder: what more could lie in store?

What is to be done? How should it be done? What are the answers we might find? Thieves have entered the village. What do we do? How do we stop them? Before anything else is done, the entire locality must become wide alert. Young men must take turns standing guard over every mohalla at night. Women must keep chilli powder handy for self-defence. This is the kind of caution we all need to have now.

The thieves may come in any disguise. They may say they are restoring temples and shrines. They may spread false news. They may encourage bhajan singing. They may even give communities idols, flags, money, and get them to drink and dance joyfully in the name of bhakti. They may bait and capture an entire community, using sentiments dear to its heart. To escape it, we must first recognise this conspiracy. This calls for everyone to be aware. The wise and the discerning must talk about right and wrong at least now. Words of love, tolerance and justice must be heard from within society.

6

In the light of all this, the secret of the anti-conversion law…

The Karnataka government recently presented the Karnataka Protection of Right to Freedom of Religion Bill, 2021 in the Legislative Assembly, and got a hurried approval. With the backing of the cabinet and the governor, the government took the ordinance route to passing it into law. This law is now called the Karnataka Protection of Right to Freedom of Religion Ordinance, 2022. When you look inside it, though, you see that it is replete with provisions that place hurdles in the way of religious conversion. There is neither piety nor freedom, and no right or protection in this law. In the name of freedom, it is out to kill. That is why, in keeping with its inner meaning, everyone calls it 'the anti-conversion law'.

Instances of local chieftains,[1] kings, even emperors, enforcing a law against conversion aren't commonly found in Indian history. India has been the experimental ground for various religious faiths, sects and spiritual pursuits. This *is* Indian culture. This *is* Indian tradition. This is what gets to be called Indianness, or Bharateeyate. Historians say wars end in matrimony. For that matter, even in our puranas, Gods fight battles, win and lose, marry, mix and live together. However, these self-proclaimed devotees of God live in a gutter of intolerance and hatred, and with feelings of high and low that come from wearing caste, sectarian and religious blinkers. Having come to power concealing within itself the aspirations of the RSS, an organisation determined to establish a Chaturvarna Hindutva empire, the BJP is marching in the direction of the past. This too is a part of the conspiracy of the Chaturvarna order of the past.

Now, using a law ostensibly meant to protect the right of religious freedom, the government has created such formidable hurdles that those who wish to convert are in for a gruelling time.

They are required to give at least thirty days' notice to the district magistrate, using Form 1. The religious leaders officiating at the conversion are required to fill Form 2 and give similar notice. And then objections are invited. Relatives, neighbours and colleagues of the person who wishes to convert are allowed to raise objections. Can it get any more bizarre? If a person is forced or induced to convert, that person ought to be the one to complain, right? Is this government fooling around with the lives of its people and the Indian Constitution or what?

Given the punishment this law lays down for those who conduct the conversion ritual, no one will come forward to officiate. Even if a person converts voluntarily, chances are high that the conversion will be attributed to force, deception, undue influence, pressure and inducement, and the one who facilitated it hauled up and tortured. So, what should those who want to convert of their own volition do? The only way left perhaps is to fill Form 1 and persuade the deputy commissioner to step in personally and make arrangements for the conversion!

If this law had tried to stop the conversion of minors and the mentally unstable, it would have been understandable. But that is not the case, and the way this government looks at Dalits and women is an affront to their dignity. It clubs together minors, the mentally unstable, Dalits and women in one category. This is evident in the heavier punishment laid down for those converting any of them. Are Dalits and women mentally unstable then? Are they minors? What does this government think of them? It seems to believe that Dalits and women are immature, lacking in intelligence and individuality, and incapable of making their own decisions. Those in the government who brought in the anti-conversion legislation should remember this—they became legislators and came to power on the strength of votes they got from a majority of these very women and Dalits. But what have these ungrateful politicians done? They are discriminating against the very people who chose them, treating them as second-class citizens and insulting them. In the coming elections, it is up to the women and the Dalits to wipe out those who have insulted them, and thus rid themselves of this taint. Legislators need to have some sense put into their heads. They must be enabled to evolve their own individuality and develop an ability to take their own decisions. These immature sorts must be made mature. Women and Dalits must become aware, and take to task legislators who unthinkingly, and without taking part in any debate, raise their hands in the assembly.

What is the government trying to do here? By flaunting religious freedom in word and banning religious conversion in deed, they have, with a single blow, crippled the individual freedom granted by the Constitution. Also, they have strangled the Constitutional right to 'freedom of conscience and free profession', which allows the 'practice and propagation of religion'. In the process, they have humiliated women and Dalits and turned them into second-class citizens.

There was an amusing incident in the Legislative Assembly in connection with the anti-conversion law. Goolihatti Shekhar, the BJP legislator from Hosadurga who rose to fame by taking off his shirt in the assembly, spoke about his mother converting to Christianity. No one wondered what the reasons for his mother's conversion might have been. Had she been so frustrated and pained by her son's indiscretions that she sought solace in Christ? No one paid attention to the mother! All things considered, doesn't this anguished mother enjoy the Constitutional right to practise any religion? Not a single legislator brought up this question. This anti-conversion law reeks of the Manudharmashastra injunction that a woman stays dependent on her father, husband or son. On the whole, what has happened here is a vanquishing of the Constitution and the establishment of Manudharmashastra.

When it comes to reservation for the economically weaker sections, it becomes apparent yet again that the Constitution has been vanquished and Manudharmashastra simultaneously established. The yardsticks used for reservation, an exercise rooted in social justice, were social and educational backwardness, and a lack of representation in education and employment. The policy of reservation held out justice. It had character. But in one stroke, Prime Minister Modi, the sole leader of the RSS's offspring BJP, reserved 10 per cent of all jobs for the economically weaker sections. As a result, the justice inherent in the concept of reservation collapsed. As did its character.

To go back a little in time, groups unleashed by the RSS led the violent agitations against the Mandal Commission,[2] the mandate of which was to determine reservations for the backward classes. Coming from such a background, Modi delivered a covert blow to the Constitution after becoming prime minister by reserving jobs for the economically weaker sections.[3] The objective is simple: to render the Constitution inconsequential, irrespective of whether it stays or goes. A section ahead of all others socially, a section overrepresented in education and employment, and a section that constitutes just 5 per cent of the population gets 10 per cent reservation in jobs. Our Prime Minister Modi has ensured that a section that enjoys more opportunities than others gets even more opportunities. This gift is in keeping with the

Manudharmashastra injunction that those at the top should get more. No need to consult an astrologer—the RSS is determined that the Manudharmashastra must shape our present. Towards this end, the RSS and its affiliates have created an atmosphere in which anyone who protests against such laws is branded as anti-national by their Koogu Maari[4] brigade. India is suffering in an atmosphere of this kind.

7

At least now…

What do we do now? But before we consider that, we must take note of a trend. And what a paradoxical trend it is! The RSS and its myriad progeny, setting out to build a society based on inequality and discrimination, are working as one. What is the secret behind this unity? It is no big secret, actually. Behind it lie the same old backward-looking beliefs about the past—the Chaturvarna Hindutva society, Manudharmashastra and Aryan supremacy— and the demolition of the Indian Constitution. These random regressive beliefs keep the RSS breathing. That is the reason it first destroys the power of discernment. Golwalkar, the guru of the RSS, has explained this clearly. When the beliefs of an organisation are beyond the power of judgement or questioning, it behaves like a herd, as if hypnotised, taking orders from above.

But what is happening on the other side? The side that believes in reason and a forward-looking philosophy, and accepts ideas only after questioning them? The side that could come up with new and innovative ideas. Organisations with such aspirations are fragmented—and they keep fragmenting from within those fragments. At this difficult juncture, when the backward-marching RSS and its affiliates have become strong, and when even status quoists have lost their dominance, the onus on forward-looking groups, organisations and parties is greater.

Creating the illusion that a petty Hindu sect—a minority in reality and propagating the old, abominable Chaturvarna Hindutva—is representative of the majority, the RSS is dragging the country backwards. Lately, meddling with the curriculum, it has twisted the feet of children's textbooks the way the feet of ghosts are flipped, making these texts too walk backwards. The gait of the RSS is like that of a backward-walking ghost. The need of the hour is to strip these regressive groups of their various disguises, one by one, and to expose their real nature to society. Forward-looking groups must wake up to this, even if they are otherwise caught up in their struggles.

At least now, forward-looking groups, organisations and parties should rise above being just little streams; they should flow collectively as one river. To be able to do that, they must abandon the unhealthy attitude that they are pure and superior to others. They must give up their ego, and develop the humility to accept that hundreds of paths might exist for attaining an aim. They must put an end to their leadership squabbles. Rather than insist narrow-mindedly that they lead, or that their party lead, they must join a broad alliance to save federalism and the Indian Constitution and the diversity that is the life breath of India. They must come together to build a participatory democracy, one in which all citizens and communities take part, and to create a culture that is tolerant, loving and free of distinctions of high and low. Justice must flourish in society. Everyone should find a new birth by being a part of their communities and of society at large. They must find new ways of speaking and being.

What we need first and foremost is caution. When the Koogu Maaris of the RSS arrive at our doors, we should refuse to heed them. Like our people in the villages, we must write 'Naale baa' (Come tomorrow) on our doors. The moment we respond to the call, and add our voice to that of the Koogi Maari's, that very moment our fall begins. The wisdom born from the experience of the countryside—that 'divisiveness is the devil, oneness is god'—must become our wisdom too.

I say this because adharma is dancing wildly in the guise of dharma today. Inequality is becoming a norm. When will this reign end? To recall Basavanna's[1] words: Where can we stand when the earth is on fire?

At this point, I am reminded of the story of the king Suraraja. He calls his followers and gets them drunk on liquor stored in the palace—Suraraja wants them to forget their problems and worries and stay happy. He wants them always to praise him, destroy his rivals and never question his rule. But, intoxicated by the liquor he serves them, they go on a rampage. Finding joy in their intoxication, and in their rampages, they lose self-control. The king is no longer in control either. He loses face among his royal peers. The king now tries then to rein in the drunk lot. But his followers, already running amok, turn his throne upside down. When discrimination and fragmentation become extreme, and law and order disappear from sight, such is the tragedy that follows. It may be happening today, or it may happen tomorrow.

Perhaps anything excessive ends this way, whether it is the intoxication of hate or the intoxication of religious fanaticism. Reap what you sow, as they say. When hatred, intolerance and superstition are cultivated and the harvest is set on fire, the blaze initially burns as intended. Later, it burns down the very people who lit it. They say if a sorcerer creates a monster called hate and lets it loose, it goes out and eats up everything in its way, and eventually returns to gobble up its own maker and burp in contentment. There is no hocus-pocus here. Perhaps it is the very rhythm of nature. This analogy of the sorcerer and the monster applies most fittingly to the RSS and its affiliates today. And not just to them, but also to anyone in their place. If we are up to such things, it applies to us as well. Let us walk together, bearing this in mind.

Afterword*

YOGENDRA YADAV

I first heard about Devanura Mahadeva three decades ago from my friend, the late D.R. Nagaraj. My friendship and political fellowship with Devanura is less than a decade old. Ours is an odd kind of friendship, struggling to bridge the vast physical and linguistic distance between us with some English, more intuition and a lot of trust. The political partnership between Karnataka Sarvodaya (an extraordinary coming together of Dalit and farmer movements), led by

---

* This draws upon two of my earlier articles: 'Kannada author Devanoora Mahadeva fills the silence, takes RSS head on in his 68-page book', *The Print*, 21 July 2022, and 'A nationalism that's anti-national, *The Hindu*, 26 September 2018.

him, and Swaraj India, initially headed by me, is hardly an example of electoral success. Yet, I cherish this relationship and think of him before taking any major decision.

It was natural for me to celebrate the instant and well-deserved success of his booklet *RSS: Aala Mattu Agala*. The reason was not just my personal connect with the author. Over the last few years, Karnataka has been seen, and presented, as a laboratory of the Hindutva brand of politics of hate. This has shocked and pained me, for I have seen and known Karnataka to be an intellectual and cultural resource for the kind of politics our country needs. For me, this is the land of the Vachanakaras, of the poems of Kuvempu and of the vibrant socialist literary tradition. The appearance and reception of Devanura Mahadeva's booklet assures me that Kannada literary culture has not lost its political vigour, that Karnataka may have imported a political virus from north India, but it does not need to import the antidote.

As this English version goes to press, Devanura's booklet has already sold over 1,07,000 copies in Kannada. Its translations have already appeared in Telugu (and has apparently sold over 1.3 lakh copies), Tamil and Marathi (two versions). Unauthorised English translations have been doing the rounds on WhatsApp for a few weeks. The wait for this authentic English edition—both accurate and lucid, with the addition of meticulous footnotes—was clearly worth it. The Hindi translation is ready, and several other language translations are in the pipeline. It is after a long time that a Kannada publication, that too non-fiction, has been noticed by the Delhi-based 'national' media, including the Hindi newspapers.

What accounts for this extraordinary success? I turned to my friend Chandan Gowda, a sociologist deeply invested in the cultural history of Karnataka, especially the socialist tradition that Devanura comes from. The timing matters, he said, what with the intensely charged communal atmosphere in the state. From hijab to love jihad to azaan, Karnataka is at the centre of every controversy, every new experiment, involving the communal politics of 'Hindutva'.

Very few writers, even the progressive critics of the BJP, are willing to take the RSS head on. There is a spiral of silence. That is why this forthright engagement with the roots of the politics of hate has grabbed attention.

More than the context, the book works because of its author: an iconic Kannada literary figure, a towering public intellectual and a revered political activist in Karnataka. Shy and self-effacing to a fault, always a little out of sorts, a bit dishevelled. His is not the carefully designed carelessness of a bohemian poet. It is just that his life has a different rhythm and radically different set of priorities than you would imagine of a celebrity.

Everyone who knows Kannada knows that Devanura Mahadeva does not write or speak much, but when he does, truth speaks through him. His entire literary output is just about 200 pages. His essays are short, his speeches even shorter, usually written, and he just reads them out without any affect. But Kannadigas hang on to every word he utters. For they know that his words are not for sale. He had turned down the coveted Nripatunga Award in 2010 and refused nomination to the Rajya Sabha way back in the 1990s. He also returned his Padma Shri and Sahitya Akademi awards in 2015. You cannot bend Devanura Mahadeva. You cannot sweet-talk him. Even his critics do not point fingers at him. Integrity defines his life, his actions, his words.

Yes, he is Dalit. But calling Devanura Mahadeva a Dalit intellectual does not describe him. It tells us something about his origins, the social milieu that he writes about and the cultural resources he draws upon. 'Dalit' or 'literature' or its conjunction does not capture the political, ethical and indeed spiritual quest that Mahadeva's words embody. Unlike many Dalit activists, he refuses to play the angry Dalit and limit his horizons to one section of humanity. In doing so, he refuses to accept the age-old division of intellectual labour that has continued seamlessly in our times. The outcastes—modern Dalits and OBCs—can at best aspire to be their own advocates, in charge of a slice of truth. Brahmins are meant to be non-partisan arbiters of truth, transcending their accident of birth, extending their empathy to everyone, including the Shudras. Mahadeva defies these roles and empathises with everyone, including the upper-caste characters in his fiction. His politics embraces all of humanity and beyond, including nature. He aims at nothing less than truth in its entirety.

This is why his inquiry into the depth (aala) and the breadth (agala) of the RSS makes waves. When the omnipresent Narendra Modi and the omnipotent election machine of the BJP draws all attention everywhere, Devanura Mahadeva fixes his gaze at the real source and centre of power, the RSS. At a time when the obsequious media and commentariat are ever willing to suspend disbelief, and eager to invent the soft, liberal gloss the RSS needs, Devanura dares to speak the unvarnished truth. Most critics limit themselves to asking questions that the RSS anticipates, indeed wants: Does the RSS exercise influence on this government? Is the RSS anti-Muslim? Devanura's inquiry invites us to ask a harder and deeper question: Is the RSS anti-national?

On the face of it, this is an odd question. Nationalism, Indianness and Hindutva are very much the calling cards of the RSS. If anything, its critics accuse it of being ultra-nationalist. Thus, to question its nationalist credentials is counter intuitive, if not outrageous. Yet, given the salience of the RSS in our national public life today, this question needs to be debated in all seriousness. It is not a central question in this booklet, yet even a cursory reading pushes you in this direction. The question is about the theory and practice of the RSS as an organisation and its relationship to the Indian nation, its past, present and future.

The author begins this booklet with a short chapter of quotations from some of the founding fathers and ideologues of the RSS. These quotes bring out some indisputable facets of its founding ideology: belief in the purity and supremacy of the Aryan race, which is as false as it is obnoxious; Nazi-like ideas of brute suppression of minorities so as to establish a majoritarian rule; a support for the Chaturvarna caste order that aims at bringing back Brahminic supremacy; and a total rejection of the founding principles of the Indian Constitution.

The booklet does not delve into the history of the RSS. But given these beliefs, it is not surprising that, right from its inception in 1925, the RSS was not in any way active during the national movement. In fact, its associates like the Hindu Mahasabha actively opposed the national movement. It is also a well-documented fact that V.D. Savarkar, whose ideology inspired the RSS founders and who remains its icon, was released from Cellular Jail after he wrote several mercy petitions pledging loyalty to the British empire. After his release, he lived off a stipend from the British government and remained faithful to the conditions they imposed on him. While the RSS kept away from the Quit India movement, some Hindu Mahasabha leaders collaborated with the British during this biggest anti-colonial uprising. Well before the Muslim League proposed it, Hindu nationalists advocated the two-nation theory. And it is no secret that Nathuram Godse was once an RSS member, and very much a part of its extended family when he murdered Mahatma

Gandhi. Bluntly put, the RSS made zero, if not negative, contribution to the national struggle.

Of course, that is not sufficient to dub it anti-national today.

The role of the RSS in the post-Independence era is more relevant to such an assessment. Did it contribute to the project of nation-building? Sadly, the answer is again in the negative. The RSS was among the few organisations that refused to honour some of the key symbols of the Indian republic: the national flag, the national anthem and, of course, the Constitution of India. It speaks volumes that the head of the RSS had to clarify, nearly eight decades after the promulgation of the Constitution, that his organisation believes in it—something explicitly contradicted by his predecessor. The RSS does not quite subscribe to any of the key tenets of the Indian Constitution: socialism, secularism, federalism and democracy.

In practice, far from being a part of the solution, the RSS was always a part of the problem that India faced in its difficult journey of nation-building. The legacy of Partition and the challenge of bringing together immense diversities posed an unprecedented challenge to the nascent Indian nation. During this delicate phase, the RSS was at best an irresponsible denominational pressure group for Hinduisation of the Indian state, opposing any and every concession to minorities and advocating a hawkish foreign policy. At worst, the RSS became a fulcrum of organised subversion of the Constitutional order, as in the demolition of the Babri Masjid in 1992. If Constitutional patriotism is the heart of national political life, the RSS has repeatedly stood in opposition to the project of nation-building.

More than anything else, it is the theory and practice of its nationalism that shows the RSS to be a European import, out of sync with Indian nationalism. It subscribes to the now outdated European model of nation-state which assumed that the cultural boundaries of a nation must match its political boundaries. In Europe, one race, one religion, one language and one culture were considered the defining features of a nation. In India, it meant Hindu–Hindi–

Hindustan, the slogan coined by Savarkar. India's home-grown nationalism challenged this European model with its futile and bloody quest for matching cultural and political boundaries. Instead, Indian nationalism was about creating political unity by acknowledging, respecting and accommodating deep diversity of culture, religion and language.

Today, as a rapidly diversifying world seeks to learn from the Indian model, the RSS clings to an alien, borrowed and fractious understanding of nationalism. Worse, its attempt to create what may be called majority separatism is clearly the biggest obstacle for Indian nationalism. Is it not odd that an organisation that claims to work for national integration has had little time and energy for an amicable resolution of some of the issues that challenge our national unity? These include intractable inter-state water disputes, intra-state tensions between regions, language issues, and differences with racial and ethnic dimensions. The RSS version of nationalism comes into play only when there is a religious angle to any given issue.

It is not that they care for Hinduism either. RSS ideologues have little knowledge of, or interest in, the multiplicity of Hindu traditions, the vast universe of Hindu mythologies or the diverse religious practices of the Hindus. In fact, the Hinduism that the RSS seeks to impose is a truncated, sanitised and homogenised version, a parody of orthodox Islam and orthodox Christianity, that runs against the basic spirit of Hinduism, and indeed the spirit of humanism that informs all religions. The principal focus of the RSS has been to foment Hindu–Muslim differences, division and hatred.

All this leads us to an unavoidable conclusion. Secessionists challenge the territorial integrity of India; it is called treason. Left-wing extremists challenge the writ of the Indian state; they are charged with sedition. The RSS challenges the basic tenets of the Constitution of India, the very idea of India, the swadharma of the Republic of India. It works to activate the principal faultline, the Hindu–Muslim divide, that threatens the unity and integrity of the country. If this is not anti-national, then what is anti-national? Why should this organisation not be charged with sedition and treason? If the Popular Front of India (PFI) can be banned, why not the RSS, the organisation that was banned by Sardar Patel as a 'force of hate and violence' following Mahatma Gandhi's assassination?

But that is not how Devanura Mahadeva wants to tackle the challenge of the RSS. He does not call for a legal ban. The theory and practice of what is called 'Hindutva' these days represents a cultural–political malady that needs a deeper cure than that. It originates in the inferiority complex of a modern Hindu, made worse by the Westernised, deracinated form of our secularism. What the RSS needs is an exposure to Indian culture and its multiple traditions, greater appreciation of culturally more confident Indians, like Tagore and Gandhi, and a deeper understanding of Hinduism itself. In one word, the RSS needs to be Indianised. Since such introspection is unlikely to take place soon, the RSS needs native medicine from outsiders like Devanura Mahadeva to disinfect its stale and poisonous set of ideas.

This is what *Aala Mattu Agala* achieves. Although much of the booklet is about exposing the truth of the politics of hatred—the myth of Aryan origins, the hidden agenda of caste dominance, the attack on Constitutional freedoms, institutions and federalism, and the economic policy that works for crony capitalists—Mahadeva weaves his message through stories. He draws upon the 'Naale Baa' (Come Tomorrow) ritual, where people inscribe these words to ward off the witch that might knock on your door imitating the voice of a kin. (The closest I can think of in Hindi is the adage '*Aaj nagad, kal udhaar*' inscribed on shop counters to ward off credit-seekers.) Howling demons are around, out to destroy our civilisation, and they have hidden their prana in a bird seven seas away (similar to the story about a king whose life resided in a parrot), the book warns us. We must inscribe 'naale baa' on the front door of our homes, just as our ancestors did.

Devanura Mahadeva's truth is not that of an evidence-driven historian's or a data-cruncher's. His critique of the RSS is not a replay of the secular ideological polemics. Rajendra Chenni, a student of English and Kannada literature, and an old associate of the author's, reminded me that Devanura weaves his truth through fables and folklores, through myths and metaphors, breaking open the prison of 'realism' that had trapped much of Dalit literature. He provides a new language, rich in its depth and breadth, to the culturally anaemic politics of Indian secularism. His book breaks down the divide between creative and political writing, just as his novel *Kusumabale* had breached the divide between prose and verse. Unlike much of politically committed literature, Devanura does not use his creative genius for political rhetoric, or to embellish the truth through flowery exaggeration. He takes to creative political writing as a path to discovery of the truth. He does not use the language of political theory or high Constitutionalism to combat the politics of hate. He speaks to people in their language, their metaphors and through their cultural memories. This is what secular politics needs to do today.

If this booklet has a spiritual message, it is this: 'Divisiveness is a demon and unity is God.'

And its central political message is: 'forward-looking groups, organisations and parties should rise above being little streams; they should flow collectively as one river'. I hope the English edition of this booklet, and its editions in other Indian languages, will carry both these messages to every Indian and to everyone who cares for India.

Jayaprakash Jayanti, 11 October 2022
Bharat Jodo Yatra, Karnataka

Notes

Foreword

1. Rakshit S. Ponnathpur, 'Devanuru Mahadeva's new Kannada book is a bestseller and the Sangh is fuming', *The News Minute*, 19 July 2022, https://www.thenewsminute.com/article/devanuru-mahadeva-s-new-kannada-book-bestseller-and-sangh-fuming-165974.

Chapter 1.   Where is the RSS's life breath hidden away?

1. Translator's note: K.B. (Keshav Baliram) Hedgewar founded the RSS in Nagpur in 1925. He was its first sarsanghchalak, or chief/head.

2. Translator's note: A leading figure of the Hindu Mahasabha, V.D. (Vinayak Damodar) Savarkar is said to have developed the political theory of Hindutva. His tract *Hindutva: Who Is a Hindu* (originally titled *Essentials of Hindutva*) is a foundational text for the Hindutva ideology.

3. Translator's note: M.S. (Madhav Sadashivrao) Golwalkar, the second sarsanghchalak of the RSS, is popularly referred to as Guruji among Sangh members.

4. M.S. Golwalkar, *Bunch of Thoughts*, Vikrama Prakashana, Bengaluru, Fourth impression, December 1968, pp. 24–5.

5. V.D. Savarkar, 'Women in Manusmriti', *Savarkar Samagra*: Vol. 4 (a collection of Savarkar's writings in Hindi), Prabhat, Delhi, vol. 4, p. 415.

6. Ibid., p. 9. This is not a surprising view. The English-language magazine of the RSS, *Organiser*, had this to say when the Constituent Assembly finalised the Indian Constitution: 'But in our Constitution, there is no mention of the unique constitutional development in ancient Bharat. Manu's Laws were written long before Lycurgus of Sparta or Solon of Persia. To this day, his laws as enunciated in the Manusmriti excite the admiration of the world and elicit spontaneous obedience and conformity. But to our Constitutional pundits that means nothing.' (*Organiser*, Bharat Prakashan, Delhi, 30 November 1949, p. 3.)

7. M.S. Golwalkar, *We or Our Nationhood Defined*, Bharat Publications, Nagpur, 1939, p. 35.

8. Ibid., p. 47.

9. V.D. Savarkar, Presidential Address to the 22nd Session of the Hindu Mahasabha at Madurai, 1940.

10. M.S. Golwalkar, *Bunch of Thoughts*, Vikrama Prakashana, Bengaluru, Fourth impression, December 1968, pp. 212–3.

11. Ibid., pp. 437–8.

12. Ibid., p. 391.

13. M.S. Golwalkar, *Shri Guruji Samagar Darshan* (the collected works of Golwalkar in Hindi), Vol. 1, Bhartiya Vichar Sadhna, Nagpur, 1978, p. 11.

Chapter 2.   The documents speak in these ways…

1. Translator's note: The Purusha Sukta is a Vedic hymn that mentions the four varnas by name, assigning a place to each, as Devanura explains in the following sentence.

2. 'Introduce Bhagavad Gita chapter in school syllabus in Maharashtra: BJP MLA in Assembly', *The New Indian Express*, 22 March 2022, https://www.newindianexpress.com/nation/2022/mar/22/introduce-bhagavad-gita-chapter-in-school-syllabus-in-maharashtra-bjp-mla-in-assembly-2432991.html.

3. Swami Vivekananda, 'Thoughts on the Gita', *The Complete Works of Swami Vivekananda*, Vol. 4,

Adviata Ashrama, Calcutta, 2016, pp. 102–3. Also available at: https://en.wikisource.org/wiki/The_Complete_Works_of_Swami_Vivekananda/Volume_4/Lectures_and_Discourses/Thoughts_on_the_Gita.

4. M.S. Golwalkar, 'XVIII: Wanted a Unitary State', *Bunch of Thoughts*, https://www.thehinducentre.com/multimedia/archive/02486/Bunch_of_Thoughts_2486072a.pdf.

5. M.S. Golwalkar, *Bunch of Thoughts*, Vikrama Prakashana, Bengaluru, Fourth impression, December 1968, p. 113.

6. Cited in *Organiser*, Bharat Prakashan, Delhi, 2 January 1961, p. 5. Also see: Gautam Benegal, 'Why RSS has intensified its drive to create babies with "Aryabhata's brain" and "Shivaji Maharaj's build"', *DailyO.in*, 24 February 2018, https://www.dailyo.in/politics/rss-garbhvigyan-anusandhan-kendra-seminar-kit-10-cds-arogya-bharati-hindutva-nazism-22529.

Chapter 3.   It continues…

1. Valmiki Choudhary (ed.), *Dr Rajendra Prasad: Correspondence and Select Documents*: Vol. 9: April to July 1948, Allied Publishers, New Delhi, 1987, p. 73.

2.   Translator's note: The population figures for Kodagu (Coorg) are available on the Census of India website: https://www.census2011.co.in/data/religion/district/259-kodagu.html.

3.   Justice H.N. Nagamohan Das (retd), 'Islaamige mataantaravaadavaralli Brahmanare modalu (The Brahmins were the first among those who converted to Islam)', *Andolana*, 15 April 2022.

4.   I owe this insight to Dr Shivakumar of Bharatiya Parivartana Sangha.

5.   M.S. Golwalkar, *Shri Guruji Samagar Darshan* (the collected works of Golwalkar in Hindi), Vol. 3, Bhartiya Vichar Sadhna, Nagpur, 1978, p. 32.

Chapter 4.   And now, in the present…

1.   Translator's note: Known as 'MISA', it was repealed in 1977.

2.   'JP told me that the RSS had betrayed him, and that was why the Janata Party government had collapsed… They exploited not only the Emergency, but also JP. The RSS acquired respectability because of JP, then betrayed and dumped him.' See: Ajaz Ashraf, '#Emergency: JP told me RSS had betrayed him, says IAS officer who had locked up Jayaprakash Narayan', *NewsClick.in*, 26 June 2019, https://www.

newsclick.in/%23Emergency-JP-RSS-Betrayed-IAS-Officer-Locked-Jayaprakash-Narayan.

3. Anuj Pant (ed.), 'What about 15 lakh in accounts promised by PM Modi, asked RTI. The reply', *NDTV*, 23 April 2018, https://www.ndtv.com/india-news/what-about-15-lakh-in-accounts-promised-by-pm-narendra-modi-asked-rti-the-reply-1841652.

4. Rajesh Kumar Singh, 'BJP promise to create 25 crore jobs in its manifesto', *Business Today*, 26 March 2014, https://www.businesstoday.in/latest/economy-politics/story/bjp-to-promise-25-crore-jobs-in-its-manifesto-132845-2014-03-26.

5. Subodh Varma, '2020–How the Modi Govt Led India into Record Joblessness', *NewsClick.in*, 31 December 2020, https://www.newsclick.in/how-the-Modi-govt-led-india-to-unemployment-in-2020.

6. Rajit Sengupta, 'Why Modi's promise to double farmer incomes by 2023 will go unfulfilled', *NewsLaundry.com*, 16 July 2021, https://www.newslaundry.com/2021/07/16/why-modis-promise-to-double-farmer-incomes-by-2023-will-go-unfulfilled.

7. News Bureau, 'Modi govt to raise Rs 6 lakh crore by selling stakes of public sector assets under

NMP', *ABP News*, 24 August 2021, https://news.
abplive.com/news/india/modi-government-
to-collect-rs-6-lakh-crore-by-selling-stake-
of-highways-railways-aviation-and-telecom-
rts-1478029.

8.   PTI, 'India's external debt rose to \$620.7 bn in
FY22, up 8%YoY: RBI data', *Business Standard*,
30 June 2022, https://www.business-standard.
com/article/economy-policy/india-s-external-
debt-rose-to-620-7-bn-in-fy22-up-8-yoy-rbi-
data-122063001297_1.html.

9.   A reference to the Kannada poet D.R. Bendre's
famous poem 'Kurudu Kanchana' (Blind Gold).

10. See data from *Forbes* at: For 2020: Nazneen Karmali,
'India's 10 richest billionaires', https://www.
forbes.com/sites/naazneenkarmali/2020/04/07/
indias-10-richest-billionaires-in-2020/?
sh=3a87d3b7c23c, and for the present: 'The
world's real-time billionaires: Today's winners
and losers': https://www.forbes.com/real-time-
billionaires/#4a0ec6203d78.

11. 'Gautam Adani briefly listed as world's second-
richest person', *NDTV.com*, 16 September 2022,
https://www.ndtv.com/india-news/gautam-adani-
is-now-worlds-second-richest-person-3349536.

12. See data from *Forbes*. Refer to footnote 10.

13. Devender Sharma, 'How corporate tax cuts worsen inequity', *The Tribune*, 1 September 2022, https://www.tribuneindia.com/news/comment/how-corporate-tax-cuts-worsen-inequity-427269. Also see political debates on the issue, for instance: 'Are loan waivers not "freebies" to corporates, asks DMK in application before SC', *TheWire.in*, 21 August 2022; 'Congress attacks PM Modi for "rewari" remarks; asks why govt is silent on "gajak" (loan waiver) culture', *The Tribune*, 12 August 2022; and 'Centre wrote off loan of "friends", waived taxes of super rich: Kejriwal takes on Modi govt over freebies, Agnipath', *DNA*, 12 August 2022.

14. Vivek Kaul, 'Banks have written off bad loans worth Rs 10.8 lakh crore in last eight years', *NewsLaundry.com*, 23 July 2021, https://www.newslaundry.com/2021/07/23/banks-have-written-off-bad-loans-worth-rs-108-lakh-crore-in-last-eight-years.

Chapter 5.   Where does it end?

1. 'Right to Freedom of Religion Bill: Karnataka Governor gives assent to anti-conversion ordinance', *The New Indian Express*, 17 May 2022, https://www.newindianexpress.com/states/karnataka/2022/may/17/right-to-freedom-of-

religion-bill-karnataka-governor-gives-assent-to-anti-conversion-ordinance-2454715.html.

2. M.S. Golwalkar, *Bunch of Thoughts*, Vikrama Prakashana, Bengaluru, Fourth impression, December 1968, p. 391.

3. 'Karnataka students to study "less glorified" version of Tipu', *Hindustan Times*, 27 March 2022, https://www.hindustantimes.com/cities/bengaluru-news/karnataka-students-to-study-less-glorified-version-of-tipu-101648370246678.html.

4. Ram Puniyani, 'Imposing sectarian agenda on educational syllabus', *Countercurrents*, 5 July 2022, https://countercurrents.org/2022/05/imposing-sectarian-agenda-on-educational-syllabus/.

5. R. Ramachandra, 'Astrology on a pedestal', *Frontline*, 18 June 2004, https://frontline.thehindu.com/the-nation/education/article30222958.ece.

6. PTI, 'CBSE drops chapters on Islamic empires, Cold War from syllabus; verses of Faiz also excluded', *The Hindu*, 23 April 2022, https://www.thehindu.com/news/national/cbse-drops-chapters-on-islamic-empires-cold-war-from-syllabus-verses-of-faiz-also-excluded/article65347859.ece.

7. Kai Friese, '4500-year-old DNA from Rakhigarhi reveals evidence that will unsettle Hindutva nationalists', *India Today*, 31 August 2018, https://www.indiatoday.in/magazine/cover-story/story/20180910-rakhigarhi-dna-study-findings-indus-valley-civilisation-1327247-2018-08-31.

8. 'Women missing from India's workforce: CMIE', *Fortune India*, 19 July 2022, https://www.fortuneindia.com/macro/women-missing-from-indias-workforce-cmie/108991.

9. Translator's note: The author uses the term 'panktibheda' to describe the practice of caste-segregated lines or seating when food is served.

Chapter 6. In the light of all this, the secret of the anti-conversion law…

1. Translator's note: The Kannada word that the author uses is 'palegara'.

2. 'BJP had opposed reservation: Siddaramaiah', *The Hindu*, 15 February 2021, https://www.thehindu.com/news/national/karnataka/bjp-had-opposed-reservation-siddaramaiah/article33836795.ece. Also see: Christophe Jaffrelot, 'Rise of Hindutva has enabled a counter-revolution against Mandal's gains', *The Indian Express*, 10 February 2021, https://

indianexpress.com/article/opinion/columns/ hindu-nationalism-mandal-commission-upper-caste-politics-modi-govt-7181746/ (paywall).

3. 'Modi govt approves 10 per cent reservation for poor in general category', *India Today* (New Delhi), 7 January 2019, https://www.indiatoday. in/india/story/ten-per-cent-reservation-economically-weaker-upper-caste-modi-government-1425241-2019-01-07. Also, as *The India Cable* notes, 'the Maj Gen (retd) SK Sinho Commission in 2010 had found that just 5% are economically weak but not in the reservation pool. That is the number of the EWS who are not socially discriminated against'; see: https://www.theindiacable.com/p/har-ghar-tiranga-giant-citizen-data and https://www. scobserver.in/wp-content/uploads/2021/10/ Sinho-Commission-Report-2010-Neil-Aurelio-Nunes-v-Union-of-India-AIQ-Medical-Reservation-for-OBC-and-EWS.pdf.

4. Koogu Maari is an evil spirit who appears in Kannada folk tales. She calls out a name. If the person to whom called out responds, blood gushes out of their mouth, resulting in instant, painful death. The way to trick her is not to respond to her at all, and also to write 'Naale baa' (Come tomorrow) on the door. Tomorrow

never comes, as the moment a day dawns, it becomes today.

Chapter 7.   At least now...

1. The twelfth-century social reformer and saint. His poetry is available in English translation, most notably by A.K. Ramanujan and H.S. Shivaprakash.

Translator's Note

This little book created a sensation when it appeared in Kannada earlier this year, selling in record numbers, and becoming the talking point in Karnataka. Devanura Mahadeva gave out his manuscript to anyone who wanted to publish it, and *RSS: Aala Mattu Agala* received an eager, enthusiastic reception from publishers and readers. It is now in your hands in this English translation.

Mahadeva's novel *Kusumabale* is the most magical book I have read. Drawing on the sweet, dramatic musicality of a southern Karnataka dialect, he creates a singing Kannada prose all his own. When I got an opportunity to meet him in Mysuru, years after I had first read the book, I told him he was a musician first and a novelist next. (It turned out he had listened to a lot of Ustad Bismillah Khan, and some film and folk songs, while writing the book.) But that was my first point of admiration—for others, Mahadeva is a political thinker first, a leader of the Dalit movement first, a literary colossus first, a conscience keeper first, a compassionate, wise elder first…

So when Westland Books asked if I could translate his latest book, I was excited. *RSS: Aala Mattu Agala* is a plain-speaking critique of belligerent Hindutva politics. Already translated into many languages, it has caught the attention not just of academics but also of lay readers. Mahadeva spoke to undergraduate students to understand how to pitch this book. He wanted everyone, starting with people of their age, to grasp his arguments.

RSS: The Long and the Short of It is a calm contemplation of ultra-nationalism, and an anguished analysis of how it is playing out across India. Mahadeva provides an outline of the ideological and political battles raging around us, and makes an impassioned case for a more humane, equitable society. Occasionally, the political commentary flows through folklore-inspired storytelling, but on the whole, this is a direct book, with little that is elliptical or reminiscent of *Kusumabale*.

I am deeply grateful to Mahadeva for his kindness, trust and encouragement. He modified a few phrases and added a couple of explanatory passages as this translation progressed. Ajitha G.S. and her team at Westland Books coordinated this exercise expertly, and with extraordinary patience. My sincere thanks to them. I also thank Chandan Gowda for his invaluable suggestions, and Vivek Shanbhag for his insightful interventions. I also owe a debt of gratitude to the editor Sitaraman Shankar, our directors and my colleagues at *Deccan Herald* for their support, solidarity and friendship.

S.R. Ramakrishna
Bengaluru
October 2022

Giving Thanks

I carved this book out of the anguish of my very being, with no thought that 'I' was writing it, or that it was 'mine' in any way. Once it was published, the world of Kannada readers embraced it not as something that 'I' wrote but as its very own. It has celebrated the book. To me, this came as a surprise.

When I was working on this little book in Kannada, my friends, Shivasundar, Prasanna N. Gowda, B. Sripad Bhat and Prof. Kumaraswamy, saw it as their own and enhanced its quality by supplying relevant details and valuable advice. I have relied on Suresh Bhat Bakrabailu's Kannada translations of several citations originally found in English. Two other friends who contributed immensely preferred to remain behind the scenes. I am grateful to them all.

I cannot adequately convey the celebratory response from among Kannada's sister languages. I came to know of two separate translations of this book in Marathi only well after their publication! Translations have now appeared in Telugu and Tamil. Preparations are afoot to publish the book in Hindi, Konkani and Tulu. It is going into Malayalam, Urdu and Punjabi as well. I am grateful to everyone who is helping with publishing these editions.

This English translation is now in your hands. My young writer-friend Vivek Shanbhag introduced me to Westland Books and spoke to them with the excitement of a writer talking about his own book. S.R. Ramakrishna, with a taste for music, looks for comparable cadences and rhythms in translation. He has translated this book with patience and perseverance amid his hectic schedules, often spending sleepless nights to ensure that the tone and tenor came out just right. I took part in the editing, and in every step since the first draft was ready. My perceptive writer-friend Chandan Gowda looked at the draft, closely matching every word, phrase and line against the original, examining their cut, colour and clarity in the manner of a diamond merchant. At Westland Books, Ajitha G.S., who comes from God's own country, judiciously weighed his suggestions, with translator Ramakrishna also joining in in the work. This interaction opened up a whole new world before my eyes. No word of gratitude is enough to thank the three of them! I'm also grateful to Karthika, who is also from God's own country, and her colleagues at Westland Books who showed tremendous enthusiasm and interest in publishing this book.

It is a matter of pride that the erudite historian and astute writer Ramachandra Guha has added a foreword to this book. My young friend Yogendra Yadav, an 'andolana jeevi' with the potential to take this country forward, has written an afterword. When Westland asked the writer Geetanjali Shree, still caught up in engagements after her Booker win, for a review comment on my book, it was at short notice and they did not expect her to find the time. But she did, and I send her my affectionate thanks. What more could I have asked for? When this book has found a place in so many hearts, what is left for me to say? I can only express gratitude.

Devanura Mahadeva
September 2022

'Here is a searing narrative of the RSS's growing stranglehold over our lives. A lament and a warning, the narrative derives its power—its truth—from the clarity of Devanura Mahadeva's vision. And from the transparency of his unadorned simple language, e.g., "Fanaticism anywhere devours humanism."

We must heed his advice to be wide alert. At least now. Lest his becomes a cry in the wilderness.'

GEETANJALI SHREE

* 9 7 8 9 3 9 5 7 6 7 1 6 3 *